STAR WARS™

BE MORE YODA

Written by Christian Blauvelt

Contents

The Jedi path to fulfilment

Do you ever feel like you're simply not living in the moment? You're not alone. We all feel like this from time to time. Stress about your job, your family or your Padawan's uncertain future can make you feel disconnected from the universe. Or perhaps you've made the best of a bad situation by going into self-imposed exile after 800 years of hard work bringing out the best in gifted people. Take comfort in a new hope: you don't need to be a Master to find peace and purpose in your life.

Be More Yoda provides invaluable guidance on how to attain true mindfulness. You will gain insight and wisdom from the teachings and legacy of a legendary Jedi Master – without having to train as a Padawan.

SEEKING MINDFULNESS

Mindfulness is simply the pursuit of awareness – of feeling fully connected to the people and places that surround us and bind us. It's about being plugged into the present while taking control of your future. It will help you become the master of your own life, as if you are one with the Force – even if you can't lift rocks with your mind.

"Clear your mind
of questions."
Yoda

Free your mind
from distractions

Life can feel so noisy: your commute ends with
being stuck in traffic, your smartphone is constantly
sending you updates, your dinner is interrupted
by an X-wing crashing into your backyard swamp.
Find a peaceful spot – a park bench, a quiet corner
of your starship or a meditation room in your hideaway
mud hut – close your eyes, and enjoy the pleasure
of simply doing nothing for a few minutes.

"...your focus determines
your reality."
Qui-Gon Jinn

Focus your thoughts

Anxiety can be overwhelming. Maybe it's a general feeling of unease that your life – or the Force itself – is out of balance. Or you're agonising about crashing your boss's prized submarine and facing banishment. Before you get as stressed as a Gungan being pursued by sea monsters, give yourself a minute to be still. A moment of calm reflection can be helpful, no matter how high your midi-chlorian count.

"Breathe. Just breathe."
Luke Skywalker

Practise mindful breathing

Sometimes we live in our heads too much, susceptible to agitated thoughts – even if our minds are not being probed by a bare-chested dark-sider who wears his pants a little too high. But you don't need a secluded island to find peace. Ignore the cars honking outside or the porgs squawking around you. Focus instead on taking slow, deep breaths until you feel calm – just resist the telepathic call of the dark side cave near you!

"I'm one with the Force.
The Force is with me."
Chirrut Îmwe

Meditate on an idea

You might not be facing a galactic civil war or the
full firepower of a planet-destroying superweapon,
but life can still be oppressive. Reciting a simple
mantra such as "I am" can centre you and reconnect
you with your surroundings – even if you're not
a lightbow-wielding Guardian of the Whills
and can't take down a squad of stormtroopers
with a wooden walking stick.

"Anakin, this path has
been placed before you.
The choice is yours alone."
Shmi Skywalker

Take control of your journey

Not everything you'll do in life will be wizard. Your chance to leave a mark on the galaxy with a life-changing new career could mean leaving behind a cherished loved one. What really matters is how you handle the twists and turns that the universe throws at you. Your choices define who you are, but if you choose to battle your Master at a lava lake you could get burned – figuratively and literally.

OVERCOMING OBSTACLES

You're never going to get from just winging it to Jedi mastery without some setbacks. You might be thrown off course by falling short of your own high expectations, suffering a hurtful remark or seeing your own face inside the mask of your greatest enemy in the depths of a dark side cave. But always remember that no journey ever follows a straight line.

"Anything's possible.
Padmé listen to me..."
Anakin Skywalker

Be wary of absolutes

Beware of misplaced certainty. It's easy to assume
some things are unquestionably true – for instance that
the Jedi harbour evil intentions or that sand is coarse,
irritating and worthy of burning hatred. But only a Sith
believes in absolutes. Don't turn against your friends,
mentors and everything you've ever believed in for
easy answers to vexing questions – especially when
they come from a hooded fiend who solves all his
problems by shooting lightning from his fingers.

"Always with you it cannot be done.
Hear you nothing that I say?"
Yoda

Believe in your abilities

A healthy dose of scepticism is good. But doubting
yourself is self-defeating. You might not have all the
answers, but you might not need them right now.
Believe that with calm, applied effort, a solution
will present itself – whether you are choosing which
university to apply to, what job you should accept or
proving to your mentor (and yourself) that you are truly
Jedi material. Quitting in frustration is never the answer.

"...many of the truths we cling to depend greatly on our own point of view."
Obi-Wan Kenobi

Don't be too hard on yourself

Regret can be as deep as a sarlacc's pit. However, if your apprentice has turned against you and wiped out the whole Jedi Order you might reasonably think he could've had a better teacher. That said, obsessing about what could have been will get you nowhere. How you act *now* will have a far greater effect on the course of events. And never give up hope – you may yet have a ghostly reunion with that wayward apprentice at a rousing Ewok party!

"You expect too much of yourself."
Padmé Amidala

Be realistic with your expectations

An overly inflated idea of your abilities and sense of worth can be ruinous. You may feel others are thwarting your progress: a teacher gives you a low grade, you miss out on a work promotion, you're denied the title of Master despite sitting on the Jedi Council. Change what you can and accept what you cannot. Worse than self-doubt is self-pity – it can undermine everything and turn you to the dark side.

"I have a bad feeling
about this."
Han Solo

Listen to your instincts

Being afraid isn't always bad. If you find yourself
trapped in a garbage compactor with a Dianoga
creature swimming around your feet, fear will
compel you to figure a way out. And if you're
suddenly pulled towards a moon-sized weapon of
mass destruction, don't panic – knock out a couple
of stormtroopers, steal their armour and continue
the mission. Bravery isn't the absence of fear,
it's your constructive response to it.

FINDING MINDFUL MOMENTS

A powerful Sith warrior might be lightsaber-slashing into the force field that separates the two of you, yet it's still possible to find serenity and control your reaction to the situation. You can be the calm eye at the centre of the hurricane raging around you.

"...concentrate on the moment."
Qui-Gon Jinn

Live in the present

Treasure the here and now, regardless of whether you're swimming towards stunning underwater cities or grabbing the tongue of a floppy-eared fool. Think back to when you were purely engaged in the *now*. Perhaps the time you were mentoring a podracing prodigy or rescuing a queen. You probably relied on your gut feelings on those occasions. Overthinking situations can make you lose sight of the present and feel like an observer of your own life.

"The belonging you seek is not behind you... it is ahead."
Maz Kanata

Don't dwell on the past

Learn from the past, but don't live in it.
If a 1,000-year-old pirate can do it, so can you!
You may yearn to retreat to your scavenger life in
a desert junkyard, but you'll miss new opportunities
by hankering for bygone days. The past is familiar
and safe, while the present is a gateway to
unexplored possibilities. That can be daunting,
but you'll never go from junker to Jedi without
dealing with what's in front of you.

"All his life has he looked away...
to the future, to the horizon...
Never his mind on where... he was."
Yoda

Plan for the future, but don't ignore the present

It pays to consider your endgame and how you might
get there, but don't let planning preoccupy you
to such an extent that you forget how to act.
You'll never leave the moisture farm and find your
destiny among the stars if you spend all your time
dreaming and no time doing. But be flexible
about your objectives – your dream may turn
out unlike anything you had ever expected.

"You're focusing on the negative, Anakin.
Be mindful of your thoughts."
Obi-Wan Kenobi

Move beyond your negative thoughts

We all have troubling thoughts. Perhaps you find yourself increasingly filled with resentment towards your mentor because you feel like you're being held back. Just don't let your dark musings consume you or you could end up with "Darth" before your name. Focus instead on aligning your thoughts and actions to achieve your goals. You don't need the Force to accentuate the positive and realize your dreams.

"Rebellions are built on hope."
Jyn Erso

Have faith that change is possible

Forget proton torpedoes – the greatest weapon against the Empire is hope that good will always prevail. Yet, feeling that things will work out in times of great stress is difficult – especially if you feel you have to solve everything yourself after both your dad and your guerilla warrior mentor abandoned you to go and play with crystals. Take heart in your friends and know you're not in this alone – then reinforce your hope with action.

AWAKENING YOUR POTENTIAL

It's important to find ways to avoid living minute-to-minute like a scrounging scavenger. Don't get so caught up in your everyday responsibilities that you run from a chance to expand your horizons – and abilities. If you seize that opportunity you won't simply be surviving, you'll be thriving.

"You didn't think I was gonna run, did you?"
Han Solo

Boldly face up to new challenges

Something unexpected can lie in your path –
you could be laid off, face a breakup or suddenly
encounter an Imperial cruiser when you're smuggling
a shipload of spice. A surprise can be intimidating,
but don't dump your cargo and run – fleeing a
setback almost never resolves it. Take control of your
problems rather than letting them control you, and
you won't end up as a wall decoration for a Hutt.

"Truly wonderful, the mind
of a child is."
Yoda

Celebrate the power of play

If you're feeling run-down by responsibilities it can
be hard to find balance. Try adding some fun to your
day: fire up that online video that makes you laugh,
teach a youngling something new or take a ride in
a trainee's backpack. When you're a kid, playing isn't
just fun, it helps you learn new things, develop new
skills and get active. Jedi can have fun too – just
try to resist bopping a droid on the head when
he tries to get his lamp back from you.

"...now... the stone...
feel it... concen... trate!"
Yoda

Don't neglect your physical self

Luminous beings we are, but we can't neglect our crude matter, either. Working out in the gym or hiking through a swamp with a personal trainer on your back can help you focus on your bodily state. Your mental and spiritual health depends on your physical health. Exercise will replenish your mind, body and spirit – even if lifting stones with your mind while doing handstands is as hard as it sounds.

"I didn't know there was
this much green in the
whole galaxy."
Rey

Appreciate the beauty around you

Sometimes you need to park your cynicism alongside your speeder. Even a jaded junk scavenger can find splendour in a sunset on her bleak desert homeworld. Learn to cherish the unexpected pleasures you may encounter on a walk in the park, a visit to an art gallery or landing on an unimaginably verdant planet. A little beauty can refresh your spirit and ignite your imagination like a lightsaber snapping to life.

"Look closer."
Rose

Put yourself in another's shoes

Look beyond your own concerns to see things from someone else's perspective. A little empathy goes a long way, especially if you've made a strange journey from stormtrooper to Resistance hero. But don't think you know it all. Taking a hard look at how stable kids survive on a glittering casino planet can help you see that life there is not all fun and games. You'll soon realise that you are not the centre of the galaxy.

UNLEASHING YOUR MASTERY

What if you cannot recognise that someone close to you is flirting with the dark side, despite you warning everyone else about the return of galactic tyranny? Mistakes happen, but true mastery is about acknowledging your failures, learning from them and then moving forward.

"...Do. Or do not.
There is no try."
Yoda

Accept change and the unknown

No one knows where they'll end up in life, or how they'll get there. Your dreams might shape your course of action, but life involves continuous leaps of faith. Don't fall back on old habits and safe assumptions – if you're going to make a difference you must fully commit to the new. Even a Jedi Master can balk at training a new apprentice for fear of repeating past mistakes. And if faith can move mountains you *can* lift that X-wing out of the swamp with your mind.

"No one's ever really gone."
Luke Skywalker

Embrace your feelings in tough times

We all face tragedy in life: you may have lost a loved one, experienced the end of a relationship or witnessed your Padawan burning down your temple. If a Jedi Master and his sister can reflect on what they've lost while the First Order lays seige to their sanctuary, you too can give yourself time to mourn. And by facing your grief, you can begin to move beyond it. The light at the end of that dark tunnel might just be the *Millennium Falcon* coming to rescue you.

"Pass on what
you have learned..."
Yoda

Share the knowledge you've gained

What's the good of being a master if no one else benefits from what you have learned? Teaching another – whether it's your own child, a classroom of younglings, or even a headstrong, would-be apprentice who dislikes your food – is one of the most fulfilling ways to find purpose in life. You may even find that by educating someone else you end up learning quite a bit yourself.

"There's no mystical energy field that controls my destiny."
Han Solo

Let nothing control you

Mastery over yourself means freedom from anything that could control you. Perhaps there's a silver lining to being hunted by a Hutt: taking on passengers for a few extra credits could offer you a chance to reinvent yourself. Yet being a truly free agent also means rejecting the need to always be in control – a need that's as constricting as carbonite. Once nothing has power over you, you'll be your own master. But don't let it go to your head – destiny may have other plans for you.

"The greatest teacher,
failure is."
Yoda

Don't be afraid to fail

Don't be so afraid of making mistakes that you
withdraw from everything and fill your days with
long walks, fishing and milking strange sea creatures.
How can you enjoy your idyllic island life when
everyone you ever cared for is in danger?
Action must overrule reflection when the call comes.
You might succeed, but it's okay if you fail – you'll
never know either way unless you stop worrying
and start doing. That is the duty of a master.

Senior Editor Cefn Ridout
Project Editor Beth Davies
Senior Designer Clive Savage
Pre-production Producer Siu Yin Chan
Producer Zara Markland
Managing Editor Sadie Smith
Managing Art Editor Vicky Short
Publisher Julie Ferris
Art Director Lisa Lanzarini
Publishing Director Simon Beecroft

DK would like to thank: Sammy Holland, Michael Siglain, Troy Alders,
Leland Chee, Matt Martin, Pablo Hidalgo and Nicole LaCoursiere at Lucasfilm;
Julia Vargas at Disney Publishing; Emma Grange for editorial assistance;
Chris Gould for design assistance; and Julia March for proofreading.

First published in Great Britain in 2018 by
Dorling Kindersley Limited
80 Strand, London, WC2R 0RL
A Penguin Random House Company

19 20 21 22 10 9 8 7 6 5 4 3 2
005-311087-Oct/2018

A CIP catalogue record for this book is available from the British Library.

ISBN: 978-0-24135-106-2

Printed and bound in China

A WORLD OF IDEAS:
SEE ALL THERE IS TO KNOW
www.dk.com
www.starwars.com